MW01172470

I would like to dedicate this book to my children Joseph, Jordan, and Gia. All of whom I have let down in many ways but continue to work hard to try and be the mom they deserve. I am sure I will always fall short. This process is what brought me back to you.

And to my husband Christopher who has stuck with me for nearly a decade as I have traveled a sometimes dark, twisty, and rocky road toward change.

I love you all. Ginny

Table of Contents

Foreward

The most important thing to know about this book is that it's not an instant fix to every problem in your life. In fact, it is not an instant fix to any problem in your life. The steps in this book will help you address problems you are trying to solve; they will help you create lasting change if you take the process seriously and apply it to things you are ready to overcome.

I won't promise that change will happen quickly, although it can occur at different rates for different people.

The steps in this book are a process to help you recreate yourself, whatever that looks like for you.

Every person's journey is unique. There are never two exact journeys toward change. However, it is possible to mimic other people's processes to find one that works for you. We often compare our journey to the journey of others, and even though we are traveling the same road, the details of the journey often differ, but processes can be the same.

Prior to changing my life many years ago, I was not sure how to initiate the process of change even though many things in my life were unbearable. When I found a route out of my challenges, I refused to forget how I found it and the process involved. I am very grateful to share this simple yet impactful process with the world.

This book was created to help others. Not just those who read it, but those who might never know it exists. Thank you for buying this book and taking the time to read it. When you practice the steps in your life I hope you experience the freedom you desire.

The proceeds from book sales will go toward securing a facility for a community based program that facilitates this very process in the lives of people struggling with addiction and incarceration. Thank you for helping support this cause and providing a way out for those who might not have found one otherwise.

PART 1

What this book is and how to use it.

This book describes the process I used to transfigure myself from a homeless, incarcerated drug addict to the woman I am today.

It can be used to address different problems in your life: such as, changing your eating and fitness habits, your behavior, the way you see yourself, your drug and alcohol habits, your dedication to things that matter to you, or anything else you are interested in changing.

This process is a comprehensive plan that anyone can practice. I needed something I could follow that would activate muscle memory and help me change how I show up in the world, and it worked. I followed this plan obsessively for years at the beginning of my transfiguration and still practice it in my life today.

The steps in this book have become my behavior, habits, and patterns. They have simplified the change process and assisted me in building a life worth living. After having massive success with my process, I decided to share it with the world.

Please find a pen and a notebook you will use in collaboration with this book and keep them together. Documenting your process will help you see your progress. You will also need the notebook to complete the exercises at the end of each step.

This book is short, sweet, and to the point. It is full of simple, practical actions that anyone can take to initiate change in their life. I suggest you read each step, one at a time. Put the book down, ponder what you read and how it applies to you, and then read the step again before answering questions and journaling about your experience.

Consider similarities in experience, emotion, and behaviors that you identify from your own life. The details of our experiences are not always the same, but the emotions and results of our choices might be. As people, we often focus on differences with others and not similarities. But, we are more similar than we often think.

When using this book, think about how you can implement each step in your life to create change. And, most importantly, practice the steps in your life as you learn them. Don't decide that they won't work before you actually try practicing them. That is a waste of your time.

Don't forget that change takes time and effort. It is rare that you show up as an expert when learning a new skill. Something I remind myself of regularly is that it took me 50 years to get to where I am today, and it will take me many more to get to where I want to go. Not to mention, the things I am really good at today took time and practice for me to gain skills in. So give yourself time to learn somthing new.

Many of our patterns have been practiced for decades, so give yourself some grace before giving up on practicing a new tool, behavior, or action. Give this process a try, you might find that you are much more capable than you ever imagined.

PART 2

How I know change is possible for anyone.

I know and believe that anyone can change their life no matter what their circumstances are. How do I know that? Because I did it. Eleven years ago my life looked very different than it does today.

As a matter of fact, if you would have told me years ago that my life would resemble what it is today, I would have called you a liar. I was a person who always had a reason why I couldn't change, or why it was different for me.

I would say things like "yes, that might be true for you, but you don't understand what life was like for me…". Or, "… happened to me and I will never recover from that."

The list goes on with the excuses I made and the messages I said to convince myself that change was not possible and why it would never work for me, even though I hadn't given much effort to actually create change in my life.

I experienced a series of events throughout my life that caused me to falsely predict my future and live in fear and inaction.

Not trying to rise above my environment was the norm for me after my adolescence. I decided to become just like everyone else. My environment was destructive, violent, and full of drugs from a very young age.

I had given up on myself pretty early on, long before I ever knew what I was actually capable of accomplishing. I chose to exist in an environment that was not serving my highest self. I didn't even know what that meant for years. This was long before the internet came out.

I often ponder how different my life would be if I was growing up in today's world. It is hard being an adult in this environment, let alone growing up in it.

There are so many narratives that support the idea that people are not good enough, and that we are incapable. We are living in a time when it is common to look at the lives of others and view ourselves as inadequate based on the small excerpts of a person's life we see on social media.

We often see ourselves as "less than" or not like "those people." Insecurity is a common human trait, but in the days of social media and the internet, it has become self-destructive thinking on steroids.

Because our world is entrenched in social media, people are falling victim to unrealistic perceptions and severe depression, which often translates into personal inaction all because of the screens we have in our faces.

We fail to realize that what we are witnessing much of the time is an illusion. These small moments that are captured in a narrative or photo are not representative of a person's daily experiences, and they are not reality.

I am here to tell you that massive and transfigurative change is possible. It begins by believing that you can do it. The truth is, if I can change everything about my life, so can you.

This is not a book about instant results. I won't lie to you and tell you that after purchasing my 30-day program, you will become fit and perfect in three weeks. I won't tell you that if you take a pill, you will lose 30 pounds in a month.

What I will tell you is that if you commit to making incremental changes in your life, you will see results you want if you just stick with these changes. How do I know? Because it has worked for me.

I did not grow up well rounded and start writing short books on how to transfigure your life without having done the work myself. I am truly the real deal. I grew up in poverty with violent, addicted parents. I am a person that crawled out of the depths of hell by my fingernails and made the decision to say "game over" and changed my life despite the challenges that were stacked against me.

I think it is important to mention that I spent a very long time in hell before finding the door. My personal transfiguration did not take shape until the age of 40. Life does not have to be painful for that many years.

If you are 40 or older now and think you can't change your life, you have been lying to yourself. But don't fret, this process works for lying to yourself too! There is hope. Just keep reading.

Anyone that follows me on social media knows a bit about my life. For those who don't, I will tell you a little about myself.

I was sure I was going to die by the age of 25 until I ended up in prison the second time which prolonged my life a bit. I certainly did not think I would make it to 50 because the odds were not in my favor. But, I turned 50 on October 12, 2022. That in itself is a miracle.

I am a recovering drug addict who nearly destroyed my own life and the lives of many others in the pursuit of addiction, even though I watched drugs and violence nearly annihilate my family growing up. I was the person you see today on the side of the road who looks like they will never have the chance at a normal life because they have been destroyed by addiction and homelessness.

You might think to yourself, "So what? What does this have to do with me?" This is actually a big deal for everyone because it sends a direct message that if I can transfigure my life, anyone can. You just have to choose the process and stick with it.

Addiction to substances, violence, abuse, fast living, and destruction ravaged my life for many years. Today, those things do not have a place in my life at all, aside from trying to help other people get out of them. But I did not change my life overnight.

I have been separate from that insane life for 10 years and living a life I never in a million years thought possible. I was 90% sure that I would die at the end of someone's gun for many years.

Today I am actually working on a plan for retirement that does not involve prison time, public housing vouchers, or food stamps. This is a reality for me today because I was willing to do a tremendously hard thing and face myself and the areas of my life that caused me problems for so many years.

I used drugs for much of my life. I was the kind of drug addict that would completely destroy anything that mattered to me in the pursuit of the "next fix" or to escape my circumstances. My intention was not to destroy everything, it was to stay high and blot out the reality of my past and present.

But the results of that one action, staying high, had a ripple effect that destroyed everything I cared about – My family, my kids, my sanity, and my mental health.

I would go away for months thinking I was saving people from the insanity of my life, but I was destroying the lives of my kids and my family members by doing that.

The crazy thing about my life back then was I had little awareness of the level of destruction and damage I created. I had no idea how blind I was for a very long time. In many situations where I thought I was helping, I was often causing harm.

I never planned on becoming an addict, but that is how things turned out. I was completely opposed to drugs when I was a child; my dad was arrested right in front of me and went to prison when I was four, which is when I learned he was using drugs.

I wanted nothing to do with drugs, I was certain they were the reason my dad was taken from me. For many years I was not aware that my parents were addicts or that drugs were so present from the time I was born. I became aware as I got older. By then, I was becoming just like them.

I saw that drugs attracted chaos before ever using them because of my dad, and despite my best intentions, I ended up in a relationship with drugs myself.

For some crazy reason, my mom convinced me to use drugs with her and my brothers one night. I did not want to participate, so I cried and pleaded for them not to make me do drugs. I wanted nothing to do with the drugs, but after some intense convincing, I gave in to the pressure and chose to use with my family.

They were all so excited when I finally gave in; they were being so nice to me. That's when I realized that joining them was a good idea. It made me feel like I was a part of something. I sought acceptance and love from them more than I wanted to do the right thing.

After the first time I used drugs, it was off to the races. The acceptance I experienced after using drugs was delightful. It felt so good to be accepted for once. I was finally treated like I mattered and was part of the family. I didn't experience this often, so when I was loved and accepted for choosing this, it sent a very solid message to my brain "ignore your inner voice and choose acceptance because doing what you believe is right will not serve you well with others!"

Acceptance from others was very important to me. I did not like the way it felt to be different and not accepted. This experience led me to destructive habits and patterns for years to come.

By the time I was in the 6th grade, I went from being a mild-mannered high achiever to a drug addict with an anger problem. I did not see myself clearly and did not know that this was becoming a pattern in my life. I had no idea this would be my truth, and that I had become my environment.

The years unfolded in dangerous and destructive ways, leading me down a path that I did not foresee. I stopped going to school for the most part and turned my back on everything that once mattered to me: academics, sports, and friends.

I settled into a life of destruction and became everything I said I would not. I abandoned my dreams, goals, and opportunities early on until one day I stood in a jail cell looking into my own eyes and despising the woman looking back at me.

I spent nearly 30 years in the insane cycle of active addiction. I served three separate terms in prison, two with my mother.

I was a victim, a perpetrator, and a failure in every sense of the word. I let my children down, which was the most devastating choice of them all and I hated myself because of it.

I attempted recovery a couple of different times but was not grasping the fundamentals necessary to stay committed. Anytime something was hard, I caved in and used drugs again.

I thought for years that a stable, clean life would never happen for me. I just didn't think I had what it took.

Patterns that have been practiced for decades can be very hard to break; for a long time, I truly believed it was impossible.

In December of 2012, I found myself at the age of 40 facing a fourth prison term and realized that the author of my story, both past and present, was me.

As much as I chose to blame people and circumstances in my life for my reality, the truth was, no one was standing in that cell with me. It was just me. No one forced me to make the decisions that destroyed so many things in my life. They were my choices that placed me in that situation and every single situation leading up to this point in my life. That was the moment I knew that if I wanted to live a different life, I had to do different things.

I didn't know how I would make it happen, but I knew I was going to and that is exactly what I did. From that moment on, I decided to live differently. It did not matter if my process started in jail, prison, or on the streets. I was done destroying my life.

I knew that if I wanted something different, I had to do something different. So one small decision at a time, I began choosing differently than I would have in the past. Day by day, my life started to change.

First, I chose to change my relationship with drugs. Next, I focused on my mental health and finally, my fitness and health. The list continued to grow. Today my life is unlike anything I could have ever imagined because I committed to making changes beginning with one choice at a time.

Over the years I picked up different things through reading, recovery programs, prison therapy, 12-step literature, and other places. I learned several things and then I began implementing things that worked to create the changes in my life I was seeking.

The process I implemented is simple, but not always easy. I want to share what I put in place that led me to the life I live today. It is not an extraordinary process; it is something that anyone can do, and it all starts with a few simple steps I will lay out in the following sections.

I hope this process is as meaningful for you as it has been for me. It has taken me from being a homeless drug addict to a flourishing community pillar that supports and influences growth and change in many others in our world today.

PART 3

The steps to create lasting change.

Many people shy away from or attempt to completely avoid anything that is change-related. The fact is, avoiding change is not realistic, nor is it possible. Change is one of the things in this life you can't get away from. I have heard over and over again how people "hate change!"

I was one of those people until it dawned on me that change is constantly happening. Change is like death, and no one is able to avoid it. Energy spent trying to stay away from change is wasted energy that could be used to lean into the discomfort of change.

Consider the weather, it is constantly changing. Sometimes, you don't know from one moment to the next what is going to happen. The weatherman says one thing and mother nature does the exact opposite.

Trying to deny or ignore that kind of change is foolish. If you pretend that the sun is out when it is raining, you are still going to get wet. Adapting is as easy as owning an umbrella or a raincoat and having it handy when it rains.

It really isn't any different with life. Things are always changing so trying to avoid change is foolish and pointless. There are no real guarantees so it makes sense to find acceptance for change because it is happening with or without your consent. How you show up for change is an entirely different story. You can either be that person with the raincoat or the one that gets wet. Being prepared for change is a choice.

What if you chose to embrace change? What if you welcomed it? How crazy would that be? I have been practicing the process of embracing change for over a decade and it has proven to be a huge benefit to my life.

Change can be uncomfortable and generate fear. But embracing things that are uncomfortable can change the way a person approaches any situation and problem. Embracing change can lead to a reduction in fear of unknown situations and increase curiosity.

It's pretty common for people to fear what they do not know, which is interesting because what we know and practice does not always benefit our lives. If I always acted with rational thought, I would be more likely to fear the things that have led me toward destructive cycles or endless patterns of stress.

However, in the past, I walked into those environments knowingly and repeatedly. I realized at the beginning of my journey that I welcomed destructive things into my life over and over again. I held onto the familiarity of those environments for a long time. I was not fearful of some very awful things for years.

I did fear things that unknowingly added value to my life, which caused me to stay away from the unknown and continue practicing self-defeating habits with little awareness. It's no wonder I stayed stuck in destructive patterns for so long. Seems kind of backward, doesn't it?

When I came face-to-face with myself a decade ago, I knew I had to make the leap from fear to faith if I wanted freedom. That included being willing to face the things that scared me. The unknown scared me, but it was time that I faced that fear and moved forward. I do not like to be afraid of things.

I discovered that without drugs, I experienced fear and anxiety more often. After making changes, I learned pretty quickly that the best way to conquer fear is to just go through it. It dawned on me that everything I want is on the other side of fear, so onward I forged.

Throughout my journey toward a new me, I have learned to find comfort in discomfort and to see change as a new opportunity to become the authentic, intentional version of myself that I respect.

I learned that I faced some real-life scary things and stood up to them for a long time, so there was no real excuse to stop facing life now. The things I was choosing to be afraid of now were nothing like those actual scary things from my past. That is when I made the decision to embark upon this transfigurative journey toward my own personal freedom.

STEP 1

WILLINGNESS

If you want something different, you have to be willing to do something different. In order to begin the transfiguration process, you must become willing to do what is necessary to transfigure your life.

This might sound intimidating and like a lot of work. Well, it is. However, willingness does not mean that you have to eat the entire elephant in one bite. You might not even know that it is an elephant you will have to eat in order to transfigure your life. You just have to be willing to show up to the table. Nothing lasting happens overnight, and the better news is, you don't have to do it all alone.

I have learned over the last 10 years that the biggest challenge to overcome many situations is simply showing up. I have created narratives in my head over and over again throughout my life that supported not showing up. I have done it with school, classes, jobs, and social events, cheating myself out of great experiences. I allowed my fabricated narratives to control outcomes by telling myself a false story just to remain in areas of familiarity, hence, cheating me out of life.

When the student is ready, the teacher appears. I was tired of what I had been serving myself for a very long time. When I chose to become willing, I began to see examples of willingness manifesting in the people around me.

I found myself in awe of those who overcame their challenges by simply acting on ideas and not allowing self-defeating narratives to steal experiences. In every single situation I have faced since I changed my life (and maybe even before), someone always shows up to give a little guidance, even if they don't know that is what they are doing.

When I finally became willing to open my ears and listen, I was able to recognize that I had teachers all over the place and many did not even know they were teaching me.

In time, I became aware that I did not have to fight everyone and everything. What a relief that was to discover!

Because of my life experience, I was always on the defensive. I viewed life as though it was happening to me. I learned early on in this journey (thank goodness) that all I had to do was show up, open my eyes and ears, and pay attention. The rest was revealed in the time it was supposed to be.

The best thing about this process is no one told me that I had to do things this way; it just revealed itself to me as I became willing to see it. Much of it happened very slowly, which was fine. I really believe that life is 10 miles in, and 10 miles out. There are no shortcuts, at least not in mine. I had to learn in a way that countered the patterns and habits I acquired over four decades, and it was going quite well.

Even though I didn't know everything that I needed to change, being willing opened me up to learn more about myself and then change it. There is a key to the whole change thing though, when things are revealed, I had to become willing to do what it took to work on those changes.

Become willing to do things differently than you have done in the past and your life moving forward will be transfigured

No one sat me down and taught me these things. They were revealed to me in silence while I was alone, pondering my circumstances and being honest with myself. They were also revealed to me when I paid attention to how others navigated life that had more experience in these areas than I did.

I became aware that I was the common denominator in my experiences and that the only way for my life to be different was to stop doing the things that created my self-loathing, anger, and feelings of worthlessness. Then, I needed to replace these things with new and meaningful habits that were being modeled by the people around me. I had to stop taking from humanity and learn to give.

I did not transfigure myself overnight. It has been a process; an intentional process that has changed who I am as a human being. I had to dismantle the framework behind the problems and address the underlying causes of my circumstances.

It all began with my willingness to face myself. What I know to be true is willingness does not have to be pouring over for a person to accept change. The door only has to be cracked wide enough to step through and the process can begin.

STEP 1 EXERCISE

Begin answering these questions on the first page of your notebook:

- What kind of things are and have been barriers in your life?

- Are you intimidated by the idea of changing your life

- What has stopped you from making changes in critical areas of your life up to now?

- What does willingness mean to you?

- Are you willing to show up differently in your life than you have before?

- Are there things you have been unwilling to try or do that will add value to your life? Write them down.

- What are you afraid of? Make a list of those things.

- What is the most important thing you can do differently to address your willingness to start this process?

STEP 2

CHANGE THE MESSAGE

When it was time to change my life, I had to assess the factors that played a role in my daily habits. If I wanted lasting change, I had to figure out what contributed to the laundry list of destructive choices I was making and create a plan to turn those things around.

In order to create change, I first had to know what I wanted to change, and secondly, I needed to address the underlying causes of those things. This was an intimidating task because there were a lot of things I worked really hard to stuff deep down inside.

However, my life was proof that the things I stuffed were spilling over. When I realized that, I looked deeply at myself and recognized that first, everything I was running from, I was already aware of, and second, those things weren't happening anymore.

I knew since the age of 15 that I was a drug addict and that I had poor problem-solving skills. I also knew that I made consistent choices that landed me in jail, prison, and domestic violence relationships.

But what I did not know or understand was why I chose to do things over and over again when I hated the results attached to them.

For the longest time, I thought life was happening to me. It seemed to me that life and the people in it were involved in a big orchestrated scheme focused on doing me in.

I saw myself as a victim and in a negative light when I was arrested the last time. I recall looking at myself in the mirror and being repulsed by what I saw.

I was repeating the messages I heard for many years out loud to myself. I saw myself in a mirror and said "you are a disgusting failure." It was at that moment I realized that my self-talk was seriously flawed.

It dawned on me that if I wanted to live differently and if I wanted to be successful, I was going to have to treat myself differently. If I continued to talk to myself in a dehumanizing way, I would continue to treat myself in the same way I had been treating myself for many years. The way I treated myself was the way others treated me for a long time.

The treatment I gave to myself helped me to be very comfortable with the self-abuse that played out in self-destructive ways in my life. Some of the things I did to remind myself how much I did not respect myself were engaging in promiscuous behavior, allowing others to treat me poorly, using drugs, treating myself poorly, abandoning my children, and victimizing people in society for my addiction.

It is my belief that I can only treat others as well as I treat myself. If I am harmful and hateful toward me, I am surely capable of being harmful and hateful toward someone else.

It is a common human trait to tell ourselves things that are counterproductive and untrue. I did this consistently until I believed the things I said to myself. I realized that if I wanted to recreate myself, I would have to change the message I was saying to myself.

For a moment, this seemed impossible. How would I accomplish this task? Is it even possible to truly change your personal messaging? I decided it was totally possible and that I was going to accomplish this goal. I became excited at the possibility and began mapping out a plan.

Our messages often originate outside of us, initially. We don't manifest thoughts and ideas about ourselves until we are influenced by those outside of us. We begin repeating messages we hear and turn them into our personal messages.

The type of messages we tell ourselves often depends on what we hear, who is saying it, and how often it is said. The things our family members tell us over and over again are good examples of this.

In some cases, the messages are beneficial, and in others, the messages are destructive, hurtful, and untrue. The lies we hear repeated to us become our narratives when we consent to tell them to ourselves. This is often an unseen process that happens with little awareness.

When I realized the things I repeated to myself were not things I remember believing about myself when I was young, I decided that I could reset my thinking with the same process to create a new narrative. I would simply begin saying things to myself out loud that countered the negative messages I heard for years and adopted as mine.

I thought that I might look silly doing this out loud in front of people while in jail, but what did I have to lose? Absolutely nothing. I mean, after all, I was on the streets before I was arrested, strung out on drugs, and committing crimes. I hated myself.

The worst thing that could happen if nothing changed is people looking at me like I am a fool. It seemed they probably already saw me that way so none of it really mattered. If it worked, I might actually gain some self-respect. If it didn't, I would be right back at square one.

The first thing I did (you can actually do this too) was write down the negative things I was saying to myself on one side of a sheet of paper. Then, on the other side, I wrote the opposite phrase, word, or statement. After I got my list together, I began reading the list of positive things (the other side of the paper) to myself out loud in the mirror.

At first, it felt unnatural. I felt like I was lying to myself, but I reminded myself that I had been lying to myself for years when repeating things that were not true. This process was really no different than how it all started. I was just older and more aware of what I was doing; it felt foreign when telling myself things such as, "you are worthy of love." But the more I practiced this process, the easier it became.

Changing the message has carried me for the past 10 years. It was the glue in my foundation that showed me I am responsible for my own well-being. Once I began treating myself with love and respect, I did the same with everyone around me.

STEP 2 EXERCISE

- Get your notebook and spend two entire days documenting the negative things you say to yourself, the words you use to describe yourself, and how often you allow yourself to give up on things you are doing.

- On day three, assess your list and create a new list with the opposite messages. For example, instead of saying, "I am fat", exchange it with, "I am fit". Or, instead of saying, "I am ugly", say, "I am beautiful".

These things may feel like lies at first, but the more you read them out loud in the mirror, the less uncomfortable they become. The more you change your messaging, the more you treat yourself in a loving way.

There are times when we talk poorly to ourselves. It is a common human behavior. This exercise is an active and intentional process to counteract the thinking that supports our internal messaging.

- Keep writing as you discover more. Become intentional in your self-talk.
- Read the positives to yourself out loud in the mirror in the morning, and at night.

Eventually, you have to look at yourself, your eyes, and be sincere. It is normal to cry when you feel the love you have for yourself.

STEP 3

EMBRACE AWARENESS

As I began the process of changing the things I say to myself, I became more aware of the things negatively impacting my life. For example, when I said "you are a good mom", I had to recognize where I fell short of being a good mom and become willing to change those things.

At this point, the steps in this process begin to overlap. Once awareness is accessed, it is time to dig into willingness (Step #1) and make a decision to address the things that are being revealed.

What does this mean? It means doing whatever it takes to become someone I respect. Another clear example is when I began telling myself that I was honest and trustworthy and then realizing that an automatic response of mine was not telling the truth and justifying why 'white lies' are ok. Then, honestly telling myself that if I want to be someone I respect, I must act in a respectful manner.

That is when I dug into the discomfort and insecurity of uncovering those truths and became honest with myself that I must do something different if I wanted to truly become the person I was speaking into existence.

As I began saying positive things about myself and to myself and replaced the negative self-talk with loving positive language, I gained awareness of how I was falling short of showing up as the person I was actively working to become. With my emerging awareness, I found the willingness to address the things that were being revealed to me as I paid closer attention.

Awareness is not always the result of personal revelation; it sometimes comes in the form of an externally-shared perspective. When someone is impacted by my behavior and they take the time to let me know how I affected them, this can also create awareness if I am willing to listen.

In the past, I had an automatic response to many of these situations which went something like, "I really don't care what others have to say." As I grew as an individual, I became willing to listen to other people's perspectives and opinions. When I listen to others, I can assess the situation and decide whether or not I am responsible for the effect my behavior has had on their lives. When I am unsure if I am responsible, I call someone I respect who isn't involved in the situation and ask for their opinion and go from there.

The more I am willing to adopt awareness, the more open I become. The more willing I am to assess situations in my life, the more willing I am to be responsible for my part in things.

No matter how uncomfortable truths that we experience about ourselves can feel, the fact of the matter is, the more aware we are of our harmful behavior, the more likely we are to change it.

Embracing awareness has given me the opportunity to work on the things I have seen in myself that I do not respect or like, and reconstruct how I show up in the world.

I have recognized that not all things that are uncomfortable need to change. I have also learned that my choices and behaviors have enabled me to meet my needs over the years and that I am not all bad nor have "I got this" in every area of my life. I have gained a tremendous amount of self-respect and confidence by adopting this step and choosing to allow myself to be human and create change in the areas that have caused me and others in my life pain.

STEP 3 EXERCISE

Get that notebook out and start answering the questions for step 3.

- What have you become aware of about yourself so far in this journey that you either ignored in the past or simply did not see?

- Are the things you have become aware of hindering your ability to succeed in the way you want to?

- Are you willing to address the things that are not serving you?

- What are some things you can do to maintain awareness in these areas?

- Are there some areas of awareness that are more important to focus on than others?

- What are those things?

- Will you invite others you trust to share their perspective with you?

STEP 4

TAKE RESPONSIBILITY

Taking responsibility can be a very hard task, especially when I feel justified in my behavior. For years, I believed that the choices I made were justified because of the things that happened to me throughout my life.

The thing I did not realize for many years is that the choices I was making hurt me and my children, not the people that did things to me. When I became aware that the people who hurt me were not the ones paying the consequences for the choices I made, I realized the choices that were harming me were mine and mine alone.

This was a breakthrough moment in my life. This is when I knew it was time to take responsibility for the things that were making my life harder than it needed to be.

Taking responsibility for my life was not easy; it happened one moment of clarity at a time. This can be a very slow process, kind of like watching a glacier melt.

For years, I blamed everyone and everything else for my moral and physical failings in life. When I was sitting in jail booking the last time, I knew something had to change.

The reality for me is there was no one else there with me, it was just me looking at myself in the mirror. My mom wasn't there, my ex-husband wasn't there, and the people that stole from me weren't there. It was just me, all by myself. That is when I knew it was time for Ginny to grow up and take responsibility. Otherwise, I was destined for an even longer life of misery.

Over the years, I gained a lot of insight into what not to do. But as I began this transfigurative process, I knew that I had what it takes to recreate myself. This would be a brand new journey but one that I was sure I could travel successfully through. I mean, what did I have to lose?

I pretty much lost everything over the past 40 years, including my self-respect. It seemed the worst thing that could happen is I would be right here at the same place I was very familiar with if this idea didn't work. So I began my new process.

The first thing I had to do was to become willing to look at myself, and then willing to be honest about what I saw if I wanted to overcome my fear and take responsibility.

As I practiced the previous three steps, becoming willing, changing the message, and embracing awareness, I knew the next thing to do would be to take responsibility and change my behavior. This has not been a fast process. My changes did not take place overnight. It took a long time for me to acquire the habits and patterns that were so destructive in my life and it would take time for me to turn those things around.

With time and patience, which I had by the time I got to this place, I began to change. One slow and sometimes painful decision, behavior, gesture, and thought at a time.

As I stopped to honestly assess the reality of my life, I recognized that the things I did not like were the result of decisions I previously made. For example, being in jail. It was my drug use that motivated me to commit crimes, nothing else. I justified the reason for using drugs and committing crimes; I simply blamed the abusive relationship I chose to be in as the responsible party for my circumstances. This relationship was no more responsible for my choices than my children were.

I had to take a look at the choices I made if I wanted to escape the patterns I repeated. If I wanted a different reality, I was going to have to become radically aware of my choices and change them.

Coming to that realization was groundbreaking for me. When I recognized that I was the author of my story, it gave me the chance to rewrite the upcoming chapters. Previous chapters of my life help me to know what to avoid moving forward. When I took action toward changing the things that contributed to unwanted outcomes, the level of respect I had for myself changed as well.

Taking responsibility for my life, thoughts, words, and actions has set me free in ways that I never knew were possible. I remember feeling like "I wish someone would have told me how simple things could be all along!" While I am sure there were people that did share this with me, I was most likely unwilling to listen to them at that moment.

It was imperative that I realized that everything occurring in my life was the result of a choice I made at some point in the past. Discovering that things happen because of a past choice gives me the ability to take control of my choices moving forward.

In 2008, I was arrested in Seattle. Two police officers rode up on their bikes and started questioning me. They had spoken with a person I interacted with 20 minutes earlier that was seeking drugs. The person told them I had crack cocaine in my possession. The officers searched me after accusing me of littering.

During the search, they found stolen identification. I was arrested for possession of stolen property. I was angry that the person they talked to, even though I had no crack, because the cops searched and arrested me. I blamed the person that talked to the police for my arrest, I was sure it was his fault.

Was my arrest the other person's fault? I thought so for a long time. But after some thinking, I realized that had I not been smoking crack in the first place, I would have never been on that corner that morning and would not have ended up in jail.

When you become aware of the relationship between your choices and your circumstances, you are one step closer to freedom. When making a decision, ask yourself: How will this decision impact my future, and what kind of things will result after I make this decision? Then, choose wisely, knowing that you are making a more well-informed decision for your life.

I have allowed responsibility to simplify my life. I have taken control of my choices and have reduced how many destructive experiences I have. My life is predictable today because I have taken responsibility for all of the things in it. Life does not happen to me any longer. It just happens.

STEP 4 EXERCISE

- Get your notebook and ink pen. Go to a quiet place where no one else will bother you. Spend a few minutes quieting your mind. Take a couple of deep breaths in and out. Shake out your arms and legs. Release the tension from your body.

- Now, pick up your notebook and grab your pen, then number your page from 1 to 5 on the left-hand side. Now list five things, one on each number, that you blame someone else for that happened to you over the last 2 to 5 years.

- Now, ask yourself, is what happened in my life someone else's fault? Explain your response.

Answer the following questions:

- Is there any way I could have avoided the situations I hold others responsible for?

- What choices did I make that contributed to the events that occured?

- How can I avoid ending up in situations that are damaging or destructive to my life?

- What is the biggest problem area of my life?

- Am I responsible for this problem area?

- How can I take responsibility for it?

You can use this process the next time you want to blame your boss for something. When they write you up for being late and you are pretty sure they are a jerk because of it. Or, the next time your roommate is at fault when you choose to sleep in and they don't wake you up before they leave for work. Or, when the guy in front of you in the left lane on the freeway is only going 65 and the flow of traffic is going faster than that but the speed limit is 60.

You get the idea. None of us are perfect. We can always take time to improve how we show up. It is a relief to know we are not the only ones that see through a self-centered lens. When we learn that things are not happening to us, they are just happening, it provides a lot of room for growth and freedom.

STEP 5

TAKE ACTION

What does it mean to take action? Well, I will tell you. It is when the rubber meets the road. It is when we put the work we did in the last four steps to the test. It is when we move past fear, past list writing, and act our way into a new way of thinking. Taking action means doing, following through, and trying our best to be the change we envision.

Step 5 is a great step to take notes on and follow through. As I said, it is an action step. A step that needs to be taken, not just read.

When I identified the things I wanted to change about my life and the habits and patterns that were not serving me, I had to take action to change those things. I started by asking myself some questions otherwise, I wouldn't have a starting point. When I know where I want to start and the things I want to change, I can then create a comprehensive plan that will be simple to take action on. These are some of the questions I asked myself.

- What do I want my life to be like?
- How do I want to see myself?
- How do I want others to see me?
- Do I see myself as I think others do?

- How do I want to show up in my relationships?
- What do I need to do to implement these things in my life?

I learned that I could do this in all areas of my life. Employment, relationships, marriage, school, food, and exercise. No matter what it is, I am able to create and use a process like this to assess where I am and take action to get to where I want to go.

When I realize that I am not showing up as the person I want to be in any area of my life, it is time to take action. If my body does not look the way I want it to, it is time to take the necessary steps to change it. I can change the way I eat, start exercising and begin treating my body like the temple that it is.

We only have one body. Have you been treating yours like it matters? I know I didn't for years and it showed up in every area of my life. If I don't respect myself, I am not likely to respect anything else.

Something I had to remember is that it took years to get to the place I was when I wanted to change; it is going to take time to turn things around as well. It has taken time, process, and commitment to become someone I respect.

It is possible to create a change process that works for you, on your own. At the end of the day, if I am unhappy with my reality, I need to be willing to take action and it is always me that has to do it. No one can do it for me.

That includes changing our bodies with diet and fitness. Yes, there are surgeries out there that can expedite the process, but if I haven't done the necessary work to change behavior, habits, and patterns, I will end up right back where I started.

I have not always been successful in maintaining what I have no experience with. The great thing about change and action is that we all have the ability to make it happen in our lives by taking that first step.

When you see that you are not living the way you want to, you must take action to create the change you want to see. No one else can do it for you. It is rare that a person will maintain or respect something they haven't put forth the effort to earn. There are tremendous benefits to taking action and creating changes in your own life.

Your level of self-respect increases exponentially as you show up and prove to yourself that you are capable of transfiguring your own life.

Taking action is another simple concept and step. Know that simple does not mean easy; only that it is uncomplicated.

When I began taking action, I showed myself that I was capable. As I proved this to myself in one area after another, I gained confidence in my ability to navigate life without having to ask permission or seek approval from others.

STEP 5 EXERCISE

Answer these questions as honestly as you can.

- What are the areas I have uncovered that I need to take action in since reading this book and doing these exercises?

- What am I unhappy with in my life?

- What would bring happiness in these areas?

Doing the opposite of what I have been doing is an easy way to begin taking action in areas that cause problems. For example, instead of eating 3 pieces of cake I can go for a walk, drink some water, and have an apple.

- How can I counteract the things I am unhappy with in my life?

- What is my plan of action?

- When will I start taking action?

STEP 6

FIND AND SHARE GRATITUDE

My life changed as I followed the simple steps laid out in this book. I began to experience relief from my past choices. This is when I started practicing gratitude for the things in my life. I was not just practicing gratitude for the things that felt great, but the things that led me to the moment of action and change.

Every hard and uncomfortable thing from my past helped me to get to where I am today. I am grateful for all of those things.

Each time I become aware that an experience is leading to something positive in my life, it is worthy of gratitude. For example, I am grateful the woman on the train yelled at me because it gave me an opportunity to practice patience and compassion.

I have learned that challenges help me to grow, and I have trained myself to identify this growth and appreciate it.

After discovering the blessings that life provides, it is common to ask yourself, "why was I stuck in those places for so long when the answer was right in front of my face?" It's also a great time to recognize that without the time spent in challenging areas, I might not have the level of clarity I do today.

Gratitude can be experienced in challenges and blessings. That is not to say that life completely changes once I begin to implement the steps in this book, but it does improve with each new and different choice I make. Each time I am aware of improvement, I express and share my gratitude.

It is not uncommon to feel strange and uncomfortable when adopting new behaviors and habits. Noticing and identifying these new and different feelings is important, especially the discomfort. It is very natural to want to feel comfortable all of the time.

I have learned to appreciate discomfort as I continue to practice these steps in my life today. Discomfort is always on the other side of growth. I have learned to lean into discomfort, it helps me become the version of myself I always hoped to be. When I have these experiences, I record my gratitude on a piece of paper or electronically.

Pay attention to your feelings; they are important. Notice when they come and when they leave. It is not uncommon to experience them in different situations where you are practicing your new approaches. Don't forget to find gratitude for the hard things and the easy things alike. Each experience brings about its own teaching. When we seek out the lesson, we can experience gratitude in action.

Gratitude transfigures lives and perspectives. In practicing these steps, gratitude became a very necessary action I took as I began my day. I adopted the idea that if something is blessing my life, why not keep doing it?

When a person starts their day with gratitude, the rest of the day is filtered through a lens of thankfulness. I began to see others around me from a perspective of compassion and understanding, even when the driver on the highway cut me off. Yes, I might be frustrated at first, but I get the opportunity to consider that maybe that person is in a hurry. Maybe they saved me from an accident, or maybe they are having a really bad day.

Gratitude has helped me to not take things so personally. I started to see the glass as half full when I adopted gratitude as a practice.

Can you find gratitude for the things in your life? That includes the things that are hard and the things that challenge you.

It is through my hardest experiences that I have grown the most. My challenges are what I am most grateful for. Without my challenges, I would not be the person I am today and I am so grateful I am who I am. I respect the person looking back at me in the mirror today.

Each day I identify gratitude and write it down. I then share it with others. I pay forward my attitude of gratitude and create a ripple effect in my community.

STEP 6 EXERCISE

Pull out that notebook again. Writing a gratitude list is a daily practice. It is essential to begin the day, before entering into the world, with gratitude.

- Sunday - Saturday, write 5 things you are grateful for, then share your list with at least 2 other people.

- What things in your life have helped you, even though they were hard, painful, or emotional when going through them?

- What lessons have been most meaningful in your life?

- When is the best time to begin sharing gratitude?

- I challenge you to write your list and share it with at least 5 people via text, and do it daily.

STEP 7

WHATEVER YOU TELL YOURSELF IS THE TRUTH

I can convince myself that something is a good idea, even if it really isn't. I think the world can identify this to be true.

When I am watching my diet, I have been known to indulge in high-sugar content, high-calorie food, which I intentionally said I was going to stay away from for whatever reason. But, in the moment of temptation, I have repeatedly made excuses why it is ok to break my diet in this situation, knowing what happens when I do.

Every single person on this planet has a relationship with this step, whether we think we do or not. If I say it to myself, it can become my truth.

This is a very important step in the change journey. I realized while working on these steps in my life that this is a life practice. It is not a one-and-done. It is imperative that I continue to practice this step, and the others to remain in control of my life and choices.

I think the idea of control has gotten a bad rap in society, honestly. My life was so out of control for so long that I do everything I can to keep it under control today. In seeking to gain and maintain control of my life, I realized that whatever I tell myself is the truth. For example, If I say I can't, I am correct. If I say I can, I am also correct.

I have worked very hard to simplify life and my approach to it. I really believe that everything has a process, which includes how I show up in life. If I believe that whatever I tell myself is the truth, then I have a starting point. I can pay closer attention to how I talk to myself and what messages I am sending to myself in the face of an experience.

I began by asking myself some simple questions. For example, what do I want to believe? I began telling myself what my truth was going to be instead of letting chance and old patterns control my life. This method of action is still working for me today.

This does not mean that I do things perfectly all the time. There are times I fall into patterns of thinking that do not serve me well, but I often quickly remember my practice and work toward changing the narrative.

Very early on in this practice, I learned that I do not have to choose the path I have always taken; I can choose something new right now at this moment.

I began by telling myself exactly how it would be and in time I saw my life transfigure. That does not mean that I became rich or totally controlled in an instant; it is still a process.

When a triggering event occurs or when something frustrates me, I can repeat to myself in my head how I plan to address the situation which helps me to choose an alternative response. After practicing this step for a while in different areas of my life, my responses and actions began to change.

The funny thing about time and change is everything always seems like it will take forever or that it will never change. Those things just aren't true. Once I started choosing differently, I began recognizing that self-talk and action are the biggest contributors to my experience in life.

I trust myself in social settings today. I was not always the nicest guest. I have control over my emotions today. I know that if I am in a frustrating situation, I can calmly communicate instead of reacting.

I also know that I am a good person today. Not because I am performing in a way that people approve of, but because I decided that I am worthy, just as I am. If I can change my truths, anyone can.

STEP 7 EXERCISE

Pull out that notebook again. Ask yourself:

- What truths or beliefs have I held onto that are no longer serving me?

- What beliefs have I held onto that I do not like but did not think I could change?

- Have I ever felt trapped by family beliefs?

- What kinds of things have I told myself about beliefs and truths in the past?

- Have I ever wanted to change something but believed I couldn't because I already agreed to do it?

- What do I want to believe about myself?

- Am I the person I believe I am?

- What will it take to get me where I want to be in life?

- Can I change the way I see myself?

STEP 8

BE CONSISTENT

When I decided to commit to changing my life, I realized that I had poor follow-through in most areas. When things got hard or uncomfortable, that is when I quit and gave up. I always had a reason and excuse for why things would not work or why I had to stop doing them.

I learned as I began inspecting my life that it was not other people I didn't trust; it was actually me. I was not a trustworthy person in so many ways. I wanted very much to be someone I and others could count on. I had let myself down so many times that I had little-to-no self-belief. That is when I committed to showing up, following through, and being consistent about it.

When I opted into transfiguring my life, I knew that to create lasting change, I had to stick with things and I had to be consistent.

If I wanted to gain self-respect, this was the way to do it. I did not have much experience with consistency, except when it came to drugs. I stuck with drug use for a very long time. I just had to draw on the same qualities I used to sustain my relationship with drugs. This helped me to seek out the hidden skills that would help me. I just had to transfer the process over to this other side of life.

I have learned through the previous steps to follow thoughts and experiences back to where they originate from. Most things I have adopted, I learned from someone else. I pay attention to what is going on around me and then I follow suit.

It was no different when it came to consistency. I first asked myself what skills I used in the past, then I watched others who practiced consistency in areas of their lives. I paid attention and followed the example of others. I was willing to do whatever it took to become a person I respected and had to learn to keep showing up for my life and the things in it if I wanted any kind of success. I reflected on areas of consistency I fell short on in the past and began my journey.

Over the years I have heard and used the excuse "I am bored with" …, fill in the blank. Bored with work, bored with the daily grind, bored with my relationship, you name it. Boredom became my excuse to quit over and over again.

When I realized that boredom is a manufactured excuse and not a state of existence, I decided that being consistent is actually hard work. If being consistent weren't hard work, everyone would be doing it.

That is when I decided to recreate my truth. Showing up and doing the same thing over and over again every day is hard work. That is why people quit – because it is hard. Boredom is just the excuse we use to get out of showing up and being consistent.

I really pondered that thought before I shared it out loud and thought to myself, that is my truth. When a person sticks with something and shows up day after day, that thing doesn't always get easier. I would argue that it often gets harder for various reasons, one being a lack of variety. We show up day after day dealing with the same challenges, the same people, with the same response and skillset. If we want things to become more pleasurable, we have to quit placing ourselves in a disruptive environment.

We move away from the person that we decide is causing us unrest. Whether it is our spouse, brother, sister, child, or coworker, we don't often challenge ourselves to show up differently, to work toward improving the situation, and have a different experience.

Most of us say, "I am bored with this situation, it is no longer serving me!" Well, what if I choose to stick with the situation and develop new skills instead of quitting? What if the approach is more focused on growth than comfort?

When we choose to show up every day no matter the circumstances and try our best to practice the other 7 steps laid out in this book, we can create a new experience. One that does not include boredom but that provides hard work and supports the idea of variety because of active and intentional practice.

When I am working on myself, my approach, my kindness, and my demeanor, I am not bored. I am in action. Truthfully, I have not had a moment of boredom in more than 10 years. I focus on improving and changing my life and have not experienced boredom since long before my decision to change.

Consistency is what forges a new pathway to habit change and personal transfiguration. It does not have to be anything crazy or huge. I practice consistency by just showing up to the table each time I say I will. By showing up, I am then encouraged to follow through on all other areas of change. Consistency happens when I regularly practice the steps laid out in this book.

STEP 8 EXERCISE

Helpful tips: Show up when you commit to showing up. If you have to cancel, make sure to call the person you committed to in a reasonable amount of time and let them know you will have to back out.
When you tell yourself you are going to do something that will benefit your life and growth, show up and follow through.
Be transparent, live with integrity, and be responsible.

Ask yourself:

- What does consistency mean to me?

- Are there areas of my life where I lack consistency?

- What would I like to improve on?

- What does boredom mean to me?

- What bores me?

- Am I bored in certain areas, or do I not want to do something because it feels hard or tedious?

- Do I have a problem doing the same thing day after day?

- When things are hard, do I quit?

- Name a time when I followed through even though I wanted to quit.

- What skills did I use to keep going when I didn't want to?

- What is the longest duration I have stuck with something and what is that thing?

- Do I see myself as reliable?

- What can I do starting today to be consistent with things that I want to quit?

- Will I benefit from building skills around not quitting?

PART 4

Conclusion

There is no better time than now to recreate yourself. What do you have to lose? The worst thing that can happen to you by giving yourself a chance and going through this process is you will be exactly where you are right now after doing the work.

I promise you that if you sincerely put forth the effort to practice these steps in your life, you will adopt new behaviors, habits, and patterns over time. These new parts of you will not be solidified overnight, but with time and commitment they will happen. It took you time to get to where you are right now, and it will take time for you to transfigure your life.

Once you commit to this process and practice these steps consistently, you will create lasting change. Change often feels foreign and uncomfortable at first, but hard work and commitment will help you become the person you are in your heart.

Once you realize that you are capable of not only becoming who you always hoped you would be, but that you are the one who made it happen, you will walk taller and feel more confident in your capabilities. You will grow an even deeper respect for yourself than you had the day before.

It is possible to be a completely new person. I know, because I did it.

Thank you for taking the time to invest in yourself and begin this

GINNY A. BURTON

process. You won't regret it.

ABOUT THE AUTHOR

Ginny Burton

Ginny's story traveled around the world after two photos went viral. One photo of Ginny was in the throes of addiction and one was her college graduation photo. After a nearly 30 year relationship with addiction and incarceration, Ginny drastically changed her life. She has dedicated her life to serving others with similar experiences. Ginny is revolutionizing the idea of services in the US and plans to use her books to help fund her efforts.

JOURNAL

The following pages are set up for you to record your gratitude and progress and the process you experience on your journey. You can use this simple process to create and implement your own process of change. Sharing our own experience can help spark creativity to create your personal journey toward freedom.

Happy Travels,
Ginny Burton

Made in the USA
Columbia, SC
07 April 2024

34077351R00046